THE BRONTËS

THE BRONTËS

Christopher Martin

1972

Rourke Enterprises, Inc.
Vero Beach, Florida 32964

Life and Works

Jane Austen
The Brontës
Thomas Hardy
Ernest Hemingway
D.H. Lawrence
Katherine Mansfield
George Orwell
Shakespeare
H.G. Wells
Virginia Woolf

Cover illustration by David Armitage
Series adviser: Dr. Cornelia Cook
Series designer: David Armitage

Text © 1989 Rourke Enterprises, Inc.

Library of Congress Cataloging-in-Publication Data

Martin, Christopher, 1952–
    The Brontës/Christopher Martin.
        p.   cm. — (Life and works)
    Bibliography: p.
    Includes index.
    Summary: Traces the brief but creative lives of Charlotte,
Emily and Anne Brontë. Includes excerpts from their
journals, poetry and prose.
    ISBN 0–86592–299–3
    1. Brontë family — Juvenile literature.   2. Authors,
English — 19th century — Biography — Juvenile literature.
[1. Brontë family.   2. Authors, English.]
I. Title.   II. Series.
PR4166.M36 1988
823'.8'09–dc 19
[920]   88–26499
                                                                    CIP
                                                                     AC

Manufactured in England

Contents

1 The Extraordinary Family

Haworth Parsonage and the "pestiferous crowded graveyard" as it was in the 1850s. Some people have suggested that the woman in black is Charlotte.

Shortly after Charlotte Brontë died in March 1855, Elizabeth Gaskell, her friend and fellow novelist, was invited to Haworth Parsonage, the Brontës' Yorkshire home. Patrick Brontë, Charlotte's clergyman father, had asked Elizabeth Gaskell to write Charlotte's biography. She had visited Haworth before, in 1853. Then she had been deeply impressed by her friend's ritualistic life in the quiet parsonage beside the "pestiferous" church-

yard; by the wind "piping and wailing and sobbing round the square unsheltered house in a very strange unearthly way." They had walked together on the "sweeping moors" that ran almost to the back of the house. "Oh! those high, wild desolate moors, up above the whole world, and the very realms of silence."

Such memories made her second visit more somber. She went again into the church to study the memorial tablets to the Brontë family, which recorded the dismal procession of premature death: Patrick's wife Maria (aged 38) and the children: Maria (11), Elizabeth (10), Branwell (31), Emily (30), Anne (29). Now there was a new tablet, to Charlotte, newly married and pregnant, dead at the age of 39. Yet Elizabeth Gaskell could console herself by thinking back on the brief but astonishing creativity of the Brontë sisters: Anne with her *Agnes Grey* and *The Tenant of Wildfell Hall*; Charlotte, author of the celebrated and controversial *Jane Eyre* and *Villette*; and Emily, the mysterious genius who created the unique *Wuthering Heights*.

Patrick Brontë is remarkable for the dramatic contrast between the poverty of his childhood and the highly respectable position he later achieved as a clergyman. He was born on St. Patrick's Day (March 17) 1777, into a poor peasant family, at Emdale, County Down, in Ireland. His father – surnamed Brunty or O'Prunty – encouraged his interest in reading. At thirteen, a local clergyman found Patrick reading Milton's *Paradise Lost* during a break from his work as a weaver's apprentice. He offered an education; soon the boy was reading Latin by firelight, or working out Euclid by drawing on the hearth stone with a burnt stick. Patrick began to work as a teacher himself at the age of sixteen. At twenty-one he moved to a school at Drumballyroney, where his work impressed the local vicar, who was a graduate of St. John's College, Cambridge. This connection helped Patrick to cross over to England and enter the same college in 1802.

He lived frugally and worked hard, winning first class honors. He now spelled his name Brontë, in imitation, perhaps, of a personal hero, Lord Nelson, made Duke of Brontë in 1799. When Patrick graduated in 1806, he entered the Church and was ordained in London in 1807.

He held curacies first in Essex, then in Shropshire. Although he always remained within the Anglican Church, he was attracted by the dynamism and concern for the poor of John Wesley's eighteenth-century Methodist movement. He was glad, therefore, to find a curacy in Yorkshire that had been a center for Methodism. He moved to Dewsbury, Yorkshire, in 1809.

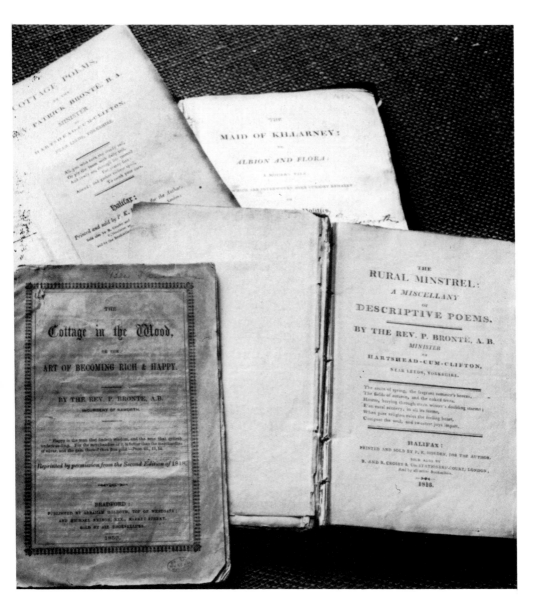

In 1811 he published his *Cottage Poems*, simple verses aimed at providing worthwhile reading material for poor families, the first of several such books in prose and verse. Perhaps it was seeing their father's name on a printed title page that later encouraged his children in their own literary ambitions.

Patrick Brontë wrote several books that aimed to provide worthwhile reading matter for poor people.

Patrick Brontë rose from a poor Irish background to study at Cambridge and to enter the Church. This anonymous portrait shows him as a young clergyman. The high neck scarf was his protection against throat infections.

In 1811, Patrick became curate of Hartshead, near Dewsbury. His four years there were marked by drama, social and personal. This was the era of Luddite riots, when unemployed weavers smashed the new mill machinery that was depriving them of their livelihoods. Charlotte would later combine her father's memories of this time with her own detailed research, to form the setting for her novel *Shirley*. The 1812 siege of Rawford's Mill in Patrick's parish was a high point of Luddite pro-test, which in *Shirley* became the vividly described attack on Hollow's Mill. Patrick sympathized with the riotors, supposedly turning a blind eye to the secret burial of dead Luddites in his churchyard, but it was his public duty to denounce them. This put his life at risk, and persuaded him to buy a pistol, which he kept through-out his life. Years later, Elizabeth Gaskell was amazed by this fact: "There was this little deadly pistol sitting down to breakfast with us, kneeling down to prayers at night."

At Hartshead, too, Patrick met his future wife. His friend William Morgan found him a post as visiting examiner to a new Wesleyan school, Woodhouse Grove, near Bradford. The Headmaster's niece, Maria Branwell, was staying with him, and she and Patrick became engaged in 1812.

The violence of the Luddite riots of 1811–12 forced Patrick into his life-long habit of carrying a loaded pistol. Here a Yorkshire manufacturer is shot by Luddite protesters in 1812.

Almost all we know of Maria Branwell, who came from a wealthy family of merchants from Penzance, Cornwall, is contained in the nine surviving letters she wrote to Patrick, in which she appears pious and affectionate. "I believe the Almighty has set us apart for each other," she told him. She promises "him whom I love beyond all others" that "it will always be my pride and pleasure to contribute to your happiness." Years later, Charlotte was deeply impressed by the quality of her mother's mind, as revealed in her letters.

Charlotte's drawing of her mother, Maria, who died in 1821.

In December 1812 the young curates Patrick and William were both married at a double wedding in Guiseley Church. William was engaged to Maria's cousin, Jane, and each man conducted the other's service. Maria now moved from the comfort of her Cornish home to live amid the poverty of a rural Yorkshire parish. The first children – Maria (1814) and Elizabeth (1815) – were born at Hartshead. In 1815, the Brontës moved to Thornton, near Bradford. The vicarage in Market Street was therefore the birthplace of the most famous of the Brontë children: Charlotte (April 21, 1816); Patrick Branwell (June 26, 1817); Emily Jane (July 30, 1818) and Anne (January 17, 1820).

Haworth, built on a steep hillside, was important in the Yorkshire wool industry. The Parsonage, home of the Brontës, is clearly seen on the skyline beside the church.

John Wesley, a leader of the eighteenth-century Methodist movement, had preached at Haworth Church. Patrick, an admirer of Wesley, won his appointment there only after a dispute.

The larger village of Haworth was ten miles from Thornton. The dynamic Methodist leader William Grimshaw had made its church important in the mid-eighteenth century; John and Charles Wesley had come there to preach and "never saw a church better filled." The fame of Haworth made its incumbency keenly contested when it fell vacant in 1819, but after a dispute, Patrick was appointed in April 1820, and the Brontë family moved into Haworth Parsonage.

The gray stone house was bleak, with its stone floors, and made bleaker by Patrick's fear of fire, which made him forbid curtains. Open moorland ran almost up to the back of the parsonage, but the view from the front was grim: a churchyard, as Charlotte later described, "so filled with graves that the rank weeds and coarse grass scarce had room to shoot up between the monuments."

The village played an important part in the West Yorkshire wool trade, but was notorious for its poor sanitation. In 1850, a government inspector condemned its contaminated water supply, the dung heaps and crude cesspits in the streets. A committee, chaired by Patrick, was to note that the infant mortality rate matched that of the worst London slums: 41 percent of children born there died before the age of six. Yet, despite this unhealthy aspect of their surroundings, the Brontë children grew up to love their home.

St. Michael's Church, Haworth, and the adjacent Parsonage, center of the Brontës' life. No trees then protected the house from the "wailing and sobbing" winds from the moors.

No sooner had the family settled in than Patrick's wife, Maria, fell ill with cancer. "Death pursued her unrelentingly," Patrick wrote to a friend. When she died in September 1821, her last words were: "My poor children." Elizabeth Gaskell later reconstructed a sad picture of the motherless children: "The six little creatures used to walk out, hand in hand, towards the glorious wild moors, which in after days they loved so passionately."

Charlotte would later recall that, in 1850, at the dark time after her sisters' deaths, she was astonished when her father suddenly handed her a bundle of Maria's letters for her to read:

The papers were yellow with time, all having been written before I was born; it was strange to peruse for the first time, the records of a mind whence my own sprang; . . . and at once sad and sweet, to find that mind of a truly fine, pure and elevated order. I wished that she had lived, and that I had known her . . .

(Charlotte, letter, February 16, 1850)

15

2 The Web of Childhood

Patrick felt his wife's loss keenly: "I missed her at every corner," he told a friend. He made two attempts to remarry, but his tactless approaches were swiftly refused. It was then that Elizabeth Branwell, Maria's older, unmarried sister, came to run the household. Dutiful, pious and eccentric, with her snuff-taking, her false curls and what Charlotte called "her old-fashioned bustling black silk gown," Aunt Branwell became a trusted member of the family.

"Aunt" Elizabeth Branwell came from Cornwall to run the Brontë household when her sister Maria died. This is a then fashionable silhouette portrait.

Early nineteenth-century education for middle-class girls still concentrated on the "accomplishments," feminine skills and graces that supposedly made a girl more attractive to a prospective husband.

From the first, the children were remarkable. They had no young relatives, no child friends. "They were all in all to each other," wrote Elizabeth Gaskell. "I do not suppose that there ever was such a family more tenderly bound to each other." The earnest prodigy, Maria, was their leader. She would read the newspapers to her brother and sisters, initiating their precocious interest in politics, warfare and "Great Men." Of the other children, their nurse later remembered Emily as most striking, with "the eyes of a half-tamed creature [who] cared for nobody's opinion."

Patrick had what were then radical ideas about education. Girls were generally expected to learn only "accomplishments" such as singing, needlework and a little French, meant to endear them to prospective husbands. Patrick, however, treated all his children as intellectual equals, providing them with adult books and magazines. As a lover of Wordsworth's poetry, he felt a child should grow up close to nature, and encouraged his children to play on the moors behind the Parsonage. Emily especially loved to set out:

> For the moors, for the moors where the short grass
> Like velvet beneath us should lie!. . .
> For the moors where the linnet was trilling
> Its song on the old granite stone;
> Where the lark – the wild skylark was filling
> Every breast with delight like its own.

(Emily, November 11, 1838)

Other aspects of Patrick's home education sound like strange experiments borrowed from English followers of the French theorist J.J. Rousseau. To test the quality of his children's minds, he made them speak from behind a mask. When Charlotte (7) was asked what was the best book in the world, she answered "The Bible," and then "the book of nature." Patrick's ideas about education, although progressive, did not entirely transcend the age's narrow view of a woman's role. Branwell was taught Latin and Greek by his father, while the girls learned domestic skills from their aunt. Charlotte was later to take up the implications of such educational inequalities in *Shirley*, *Jane Eyre* and *Villette*, and Anne

*Patrick's ideas about education were radical for his time, but they included a traditional emphasis on domestic skills for the girls, as shown by Emily's sampler, in contrast to an early drawing, "Terror," by Branwell (**opposite**).*

would deal with the same problem in *Agnes Grey*. Both father and aunt gave all the children a thorough religious education, which affected them strongly in various ways. Charlotte's writings, for example, are full of allusions to "the sublime poetry of the Book of Life."

Patrick, whose salary was small, knew that he should raise his children to earn a living. In 1824 a new school, particularly intended for daughters of poor clergymen, was opened at Cowan Bridge in Lancashire by William Carus Wilson, a wealthy clergyman with a wide reputation as an educationalist. It would train girls to be governesses, a life of "minute torments and incessant tediums" (Anne, *Agnes Grey*), but the only paid work then open to middle-class women. The school proved to be a disaster for the young Brontës.

After the expansive mental freedom of home, the sisters were oppressed by Cowan Bridge. They were forced into a narrow concept of learning, dominated by facts and the gloomy philosophy of Wilson, who was described later by Charlotte as a "black marble clergyman . . . the grim face at the top [was] like a carved mask" *(Jane Eyre)*. Wilson believed children were sinful and

EFFECTS OF PASSION.

better off dead. In his books for the young, he offered terrifying tales of sin, torture and death.

> Every hour, you are advancing towards heaven or hell. Are you living neglectful of God, forgetful of prayer, and ripening in sin? Oh, then you cannot be ignorant of the way you are going . . . What, oh what will become of you, should death strike an unexpected blow? . . . How dreadful is the wickedness of many children . . .

(Carus Wilson, *The Child's First Tales*, 1836)

The girls were harmed physically, too. The coarse uniforms did not protect them on the two mile walk to church on winter Sundays. Icy dormitories, where washing water froze, and appalling food weakened their already fragile constitutions. Maria, dreamy, untidy, and already ill, received relentless punishment from a bullying teacher; she is Helen Burns of *Jane Eyre*, "as exact a transcription," noted Elizabeth Gaskell, "as Charlotte's wonderful power of reproducing character could give."

An illustration from Carus Wilson's grim moralistic stories in his magazine The Children's Friend *(1828).*

Opposite *Jane Eyre being tormented by the terrible Mr. Brocklehurst at Lowood, his boarding school for poor girls. The Rev. Carus Wilson, who founded Cowan Bridge School which the Brontë girls attended, was the model for Brocklehurst.*

21

Opposite *The sufferings of Cowan Bridge pupils, inadequately dressed against the winter cold on their two-mile walk to church on Sundays, hastened the deaths of the two oldest Brontë girls. This engraving depicts the pupils of Lowood in Charlotte's novel* Jane Eyre.

In February 1825, Patrick was called to fetch home Maria, "the gentle little sufferer," who was already ill with tuberculosis. She died in May. By that time a typhoid epidemic was sweeping the school. Elizabeth escaped, but was sent home to die, also of tuberculosis, in June. Charlotte and Emily were hastily withdrawn from the school.

The loss of her sisters was a traumatic experience for Charlotte. Friends heard her speak of them later as "wonders of talent and kindness." Twenty years later, in her savage picture of Cowan Bridge as Lowood School in *Jane Eyre*, she exacted a bitter literary revenge on those who had made her sisters suffer. The description of Helen Burns's death is her prose elegy for Maria.

At home once more, the four surviving children huddled together into what Patrick called "a little society among themselves." For five years they withdrew from the world, beginning the extraordinary imaginative activities that were to be the foundations of their writing success. Later Charlotte used a comparison from the local spinning mills ("web" means spun cloth) to describe their creative collaborations.

> We wove a web in childhood,
> A web of sunny air;
> We dug a spring in infancy
> Of water pure and fair . . .

(Charlotte, *Retrospection*, 1835)

The arrival in 1824 of Tabitha Aykroyd, employed as cook-servant, made a great difference to the household. The children loved to be with "Tabby" in the kitchen, listening to her tales of old Haworth, of fairies on the moors. She mothered and disciplined them in her blunt but affectionate way.

The domestic routine gave the children both security and freedom. Everyone loved to read the papers, especially *Blackwood's Magazine*, which dealt with politics, war, exploration and the arts. At twelve, Charlotte described how, when the newspapers arrived, "with what eagerness papa tore off the cover and how we all gathered round him and with what great anxiety we listened." When father and aunt withdrew to their

rooms, the children were left to their reading, writing and drawing, which were "the very delight of existence."

Yet what Branwell called their "scribblemania" really began with the set of twelve wooden toy soldiers that his father gave him in June 1826. These soldiers fired the imagination of each of them:

When papa came home it was night and we were in bed, so next morning Branwell came to our door with a box of soldiers. Emily and I jumped out of bed and I snatched one up and exclaimed, "This is the Duke of Wellington! It shall be mine!" When I said this Emily likewise took one and said it should be hers. When Anne came down she took one also. Mine was the prettiest of the whole and perfect in every part. Emily's was a grave looking fellow . . . Anne's was a queer little thing very much like herself . . .

(Charlotte, *The History of the Year*, 1829)

BLACKWOOD'S
𝔈𝔡𝔦𝔫𝔟𝔲𝔯𝔤𝔥
M A G A Z I N E.

VOL. XVIII.

JULY—DECEMBER, 1825.

WILLIAM BLACKWOOD, EDINBURGH:

Branwell named his after Napoleon, and Emily and Anne called theirs Parry and Ross, after two polar explorers they had read of in *Blackwood's Magazine*. The whole set was named "The Young Men" or "The Twelve." A "play" about them soon evolved into written adventures. "The Twelve" traveled to Africa where, after many struggles, they set up a colony and founded, with the help of four "genii" (the children themselves) the mighty city of Glasstown.

The city is exotic and magnificent – "it bore the character of a dream or gorgeous fiction" – and combines ideas from the Bible, the "Celestial City" in John Bunyan's *Pilgrim's Progress*, and the architectural fantasy paintings of John Martin, prints of which they saw in the "Annuals" (collections of art and literature, fashionable in the 1820s) and on the Parsonage walls: Patrick owned four such pictures. Charlotte gives us glimpses of Glasstown in her early manuscripts. It is:

> The Queen of the Earth, who looks down on her majestic face mirrored in the noble Niger, and sees the fair reflection of her walls and turrets caught by the flashing Guadima and flung with beauty unimaginable on the glory that her harbour gives her . . .

Branwell's map of the Glasstown Confederacy. Great Glasstown is on the right. Other provinces are named after the original "Young Men," the toy soldiers, Wellington, Parry, Ross and Sneaky (Napoleon), that Branwell shared with his sisters. Angria, a later invention, was an outlying province of Glasstown.

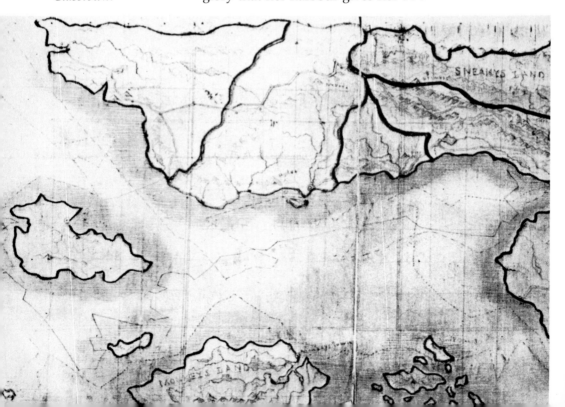

The colony developed into a confederacy of four states, each controlled by a leading "Young Man": Wellington, Parry, Ross and Sneaky (Napoleon). As the complex story evolved, elements from politics, from exploration and from the children's favorite *Arabian Nights* became oddly put together.

The children had other projects, too. The beginning of the *Islanders' Play* offers us a glimpse of the Brontës' home life:

> One night . . . we were all sitting round the warm blazing kitchen fire having just concluded a quarrel with Tabby concerning the propriety of lighting a candle . . . A long pause succeeded which was at last broken by B saying, in a lazy manner, "I don't know what to do!" this was re-echoed by E and A.
> T: "Wha ya may go t'bed."
> B: "I'd rather do anything [than] that."
> and C: "You're so glum tonight, T. [Well] suppose we had each an island?"

> (Charlotte, "Tales of the Islanders," 1830)

The idea evolved into "Vision Island" . . . "rightly named a dream . . . such gorgeous beauty, such wild magnificence." Although Emily and Anne's Gondal Island possibly grew later from this idea, it was the "burning clime" of Glasstown, and the wars and passions of its inhabitants, that continued to preoccupy Charlotte and Branwell. Their writing became a complex and constantly reworked maze of thousands of words. When Elizabeth Gaskell saw the surviving collection of these little books – "all in this indescribably fine writing" – she was astonished: "They gave one the idea of creative power carried to the verge of insanity."

In 1830, Patrick became ill. He recovered but became fearful for the fate of his children if he were to die. Charlotte's godparents offered to pay her fees at Miss Wooler's Roe Head School, near Dewsbury. She arrived there in January 1831. Mary Taylor, who was to be a lifelong friend, described her "in very old-fashioned clothes . . . She looked like a little old woman, so short-sighted that she always appeared to be seeking something . . . She was very shy and nervous, and spoke with a strong Irish accent." Her other great friend made

27

CONTENTS

1830
CHARLOTTE
BRONTE

Some of the many tiny books and magazines produced by the Brontë children.

Opposite *Ellen Nussey was Charlotte's fellow pupil at Roe Head School. She became Charlotte's lifelong friend.*

at Roe Head, Ellen Nussey, first saw her alone in the schoolroom, "a silent, weeping, dark little figure."

When she recovered from her homesickness, Charlotte enjoyed school. If it was old-fashioned, at least it filled some gaps left by Charlotte's unconventional upbringing. She impressed the other pupils. "She knew a thousand things unknown to them," said Mary Taylor, who also noticed how "she picked up every scrap of information concerning painting, sculpture, music, etc., as if it were gold."

She tried to tell Mary about Glasstown and the magazines, but her blunt friend only saw the Brontës as closeted, "like potatoes growing in a cellar." Thereafter Charlotte kept her fantasy world secret. She even

29

tried to break away from it. Her poem "The Trumpet
Shall Sound," in the style of Byron, seems to be a farewell
to Glasstown:

> The secrets of genii my tongue may not tell
> But hoarsely they murmured bright city farewell
> Then melted away like dream of the night
> While their palace evanished in oceans of light . . .
> But still as the breeze on the myrtle groves fell
> A voice was heard wailing bright city farewell . . .

(Charlotte, December 11, 1831)

In 1832, Charlotte joyfully returned to the "profound,
the intense affection of home." She could now pass on
her learning to her sisters. Her new friendships gave
her confidence; she wrote to Mary and Ellen for the rest
of her life. Ellen came to stay at Haworth and later wrote
a vivid description of the family, then at the height of
its happiness. There was the already "venerable" Patrick, with his fixed habits: "At nine he locked and barred
the front door, always giving as he passed the sitting
room door a kindly admonition to the 'children' not to
be up late; half way up the stairs he stayed his steps to
wind up the clock." There was fifteen-year-old Emily
with her "beautiful eyes – kind, kindling, liquid eyes
. . . Few people have the gift of looking and smiling as
she could look and smile. One of her rare expressive

*The "gun" portrait of
the younger Brontës,
painted by Branwell.
Emily is on the right,
and Anne far left,
though it is hard to
distinguish them.
Charlotte is next to
Branwell.*

looks was something to remember through life, there was such depth of soul and feeling." She and "dear gentle" Anne were "like twins – inseparable companions," devoted to their many pets, wild and tame. On a walk to a favorite spot on the moors called "the meeting of the waters," she remembered how:

> Emily, half reclined on a slab of rock, played like a young child with the tadpoles in the water, making them swim about, and then fell to moralizing on the strong and the weak, the brave and the cowardly, as she chased them with her hand.

(Ellen Nussey, *Scribner's Magazine*, 1871)

The family ambition still centered on Branwell. Charlotte, Ellen noted, "looked forward to what her brother's great promise and talent might effect." He made painting his first chosen career, and, in 1835, his aunt paid an artist in Leeds, Yorkshire, to give him lessons. He was not without ability. At about this time he painted his now famous portrait of his three sisters.

Branwell's 1834 portrait of his sisters: Anne, Emily and Charlotte. He has painted out his own face in the center. Branwell, unlike his sisters, was taught to work in oils to further his intended career as a portrait painter.

The first of Emily and Anne's "diary papers" – word snapshots of their lives on particular days – dates from November 1834:

> I fed Rainbow, Diamond Snowflake Jasper pheasant this morning . . . Tabby said just now Come Anne pilloputate (i.e. pill a potato) . . . The Gondals are discovering the interior of Gaaldine. It is past twelve o'clock Anne and I have not tidied ourselves done our bedwork or done our lessons and we want to go out to play . . .

> (Emily, Diary paper, November 24, 1834)

These notes, found years later in an old box, are almost the only personal glimpses of the younger sisters that we have.

On her return from Roe Head, Charlotte was drawn back into the Glasstown (or Verdopolis) fantasy. The stories (she wrote 141,000 words of them in 1834 alone) were now more sophisticated, and dominated by her favorites, the Marquis of Duoro and Lord Charles Wellesley, imaginary sons of the Duke of Wellington, and Branwell's "Rogue," who became Alexander Percy, Duke of Northangerland (Duoro's deadly rival), and their exotic wives and mistresses. All that they read from their father's shelves or from Keighley Mechanics' Institute Library was fed into the stories, whether it was Scott's novels, the *Life of Byron*, their aunt's "mad" *Methodist Magazines*, or old copies of the *Ladies' Magazine*, of which Charlotte declared: "I shall never see anything which will interest me so much again."

Charlotte's stories, "The Secret" (1833), "The Spell" (1834) and others, began to show more structure and economy, and more concern with psychology than her brother's rambling pieces. Yet the two still collaborated, creating a new kingdom, Angria, from two outlying districts of Glasstown.

> All Angria through her provinces to arms and glory cries!
> Her sun is up and she has heard her battle shout, "Arise!"

> (Charlotte, *A national ode for the Angrians*, July 1834)

Angria was conquered and ruled by Duoro, now Duke

ALEXANDER. PERCY. ESQ^R M.P.

Alexander Percy, Duke of Northangerland, Branwell's Angrian villain. He was the political rival of Charlotte's hero, the Duke of Zamorna.

of Zamorna, a demonic hero in the style of Lord Byron, a "keen glorious being."

> There he stood with the red firelight flashing over him, one foot advanced, his head proudly raised . . . Such eyes! . . . His face whitened more and more, something like foam became apparent on his lip . . .
>
> (Charlotte, *My Angria and the Angrians*, 1834)

In July 1835, the family entered a new phase. "We are about to divide, break up, separate," wrote Charlotte to Ellen. She was to return as a teacher to Roe Head, taking Emily with her. Branwell was to try to enter the Royal Academy School in London. Angria and Gondal were set aside, and the Brontës began a long, unhappy battle to establish themselves in the real world.

3 Struggles for Independence

The new ambitions soon collapsed. Branwell went to London, but soon returned home, his money spent, claiming that he had been robbed. By December he was trying a new career as writer, but his letters to publishers were ignored.

Nor did Emily settle at Roe Head. She was acutely homesick, and this brought on physical illness. Years afterward, Charlotte remembered her misery:

> My sister Emily loved the moors. Flowers brighter than the rose bloomed in the blackest of the heath for her; out of a sullen hollow in a livid hillside her mind could make an Eden. She found in the bleak solitude many and dear delights; and not the least and best loved – was liberty. Liberty was the breath of Emily's nostrils: without it she perished.
>
> (Charlotte, Preface to Ellis Bell's *Poems*, 1850)

Self-portrait by Branwell. After the collapse of his first intended career as a painter, and his second as a writer, he drifted into several different jobs.

Charlotte's Angrian hero, the Marquis of Duoro, Duke of Zamorna, a "keen, glorious being." He was the prototype of her heroes in later novels, like Mr. Rochester in Jane Eyre.

Emily was sent home and replaced by Anne at Roe Head. Charlotte dutifully struggled on, hating the teaching and the narrow school world: "Stupidity the atmosphere, schoolbooks the employment, asses the society." The long hours deprived her of her greatest pleasure, imaginative writing. She did, however, keep a personal diary, where she recorded "the divine, silent unseen land of thought." In moments of leisure, she recorded fantasies that seemed more powerful than reality:

> Never shall I forget when a voice of wild and wailing music now came thrilling to my mind's, almost my body's ear, nor how distinctly I, sitting in the schoolroom at Roe Head, saw the Duke of Zamorna leaning against that obelisk . . . I was quite gone. I had really, utterly forgot where I was and all the gloom and cheerlessness of my situation. I felt myself breathing quick and short as I beheld the Duke lifting up his sable crest, which undulated as the plume of a hearse waves to the wind . . . "Miss Brontë, what are you thinking about?" said a voice, and Miss Lister thrust her little, rough, black head into my face.

(Charlotte, the "Roe Head Journal," 1835–37)

By contrast, Emily, at home, was happy again. One of the first known of her exquisite Gondal poems dates from July 1836. It may celebrate the birth of her particular heroine, the princess known by her initials as A.G.A. (Augusta Geraldine Almeida).

> If the wind be fresh and free,
> The wide skies clear and cloudless blue,
> The woods and fields and golden flowers
> Sparkling in sunshine and in dew,
> Her days shall pass in Glory's light the world's drear desert
>   through.

(Emily, "Will the day be bright or cloudy?" July 12, 1836)

When the family were reunited at Christmas, 1836, they seem to have discussed their literary ambitions. In January 1837, Branwell sent some poetry to the great William Wordsworth. There was no answer. Charlotte, however, received a reply from the Poet Laureate, Robert Southey. He advised her to avoid the "perilous course"

Robert Southey, the Poet Laureate, who warned Charlotte that writing was not a proper occupation for a woman.

of writing for a living, and reminded her sternly about her role as a woman:

> The daydreams in which you habitually indulge are likely to induce a distempered state of mind . . . Literature cannot be the business of a woman's life, and it ought not to be. The more she is engaged on her proper duties, the less leisure will she have for it, even as an accomplishment and a recreation.

(Robert Southey, letter to Charlotte, March 1837)

Thus reprimanded by the male literary establishment, Charlotte returned to her intolerable teaching at the "poisoned place" that Roe Head had now become. When Anne fell ill in the autumn, she was sent home, and Charlotte, depressed and ill herself, and now at odds with Miss Wooler, soon followed in May 1838.

The twin-like Emily and Anne were still absorbed in their Gondal saga. A diary paper of June 1837, shows them writing in the dining room, the "papers" from the "tin box" scattered on the table. Anne is writing a poem while Emily is engaged on "Augusta Almeida's life story 1st volume."

The diary paper of 1837 shows Emily and Anne writing at the dining room table. Their precious papers are scattered beside the tin box where they are usually kept. Anne (top) is writing a poem; Emily is busy on "Augusta Almeida's life, 1st volume": the "Emperors and Empresses" are about to "depart from Gaaldine to Gondal to prepare for the coronation."

The prose of the Gondal saga has been lost, and only a list of characters and the sisters' poems survive to indicate its story line. Gondal had its wars and revolutions, but the sisters favored soft and melancholy moods that contrasted it with the fury and passion of Angria. Emily came to use A.G.A. as a vehicle for her own thoughts and feelings. Her delicate sense of elegy is well seen in an 1837 fragment about a lover's portrait and letters.

> Long neglect has worn away
> Half the sweet enchanting smile;
> Time has turned the bloom to grey;
> Mould and damp the face defile.
>
> But that lock of silky hair,
> Still beneath the picture twined,
> Tells what once those features were,
> Paints their image on the mind.
>
> Fair the hand that traced that line,
> "Dearest, ever deem me true";
> Swiftly flew the fingers fine
> When the pen that motto drew.

(Emily, fragment, August 1837)

Emily's imagery makes her poems fresh and original. In the poignant "The lady to her guitar," A.G.A. wonders why her guitar, once played by her former lover, can still revive old feelings in her.

> It is as if the glassy brook
> Should image still its willows fair,
> Though years ago the woodman's stroke
> Laid low in dust their gleaming hair.

(Emily, 30 August 1838)

When her sister Charlotte broke down with nervous exhaustion in 1838, Emily tried to take her place as the family worker, going as a teacher to Law Hill School near Halifax. It was a harsh experience. "I have had one letter from her since her departure," Charlotte told Ellen in October 1838. "It gives an appalling account of her duties – hard labour from 6 in the morning until near 11 at night . . . This is slavery."

Teaching was one of the few occupations open to middle-class women. Emily wrote passionately about how unhappy she was as a teacher at Law Hill School.

Emily expressed her homesickness for Haworth and Gondal in a poem of December 1838. She has escaped from her pupils:

A little while, a little while
The noisy crowd are barred away . . .

She uses the precious leisure for reflection. She might

daydream about Haworth:

> The mute bird sitting on the stone,
> The dark moss dripping from the wall,
> The garden-walk with weeds overgrown,
> I love them all – how I love them all.

Or she might choose Gondal, "another clime, another sky," with its moor-like landscape:

> A little and a long green lane
> That opened on a common wide;
> A distant, dreamy, dim-blue chain
> Of mountains circling every side;
>
> A heaven so clear, an earth so calm,
> So sweet, so still, so hushed an air
> And, deepening still the dream-like charm,
> Wild moor-sheep feeding everywhere –

> (Emily, December 4, 1838)

Yet Law Hill was useful to Emily in the eventual writing of *Wuthering Heights*. Here she heard the local story of Jack Sharp, an adopted boy who took over a family's fortune. Some modern scholars believe that the nearby High Sunderland Farm and Shibden Hall were the true originals for Wuthering Heights and Thrushcross Grange in Emily's novel.

The poetry that Emily wrote while at Law Hill expresses her homesickness for Haworth and her beloved moors.

41

Governesses were common from the 1830s onward as newly rich middle-class families sought better home education for their children. The status of the governess was uneasy; she was neither servant nor family. Here she is, in Charlotte's words, "toiling to impart knowledge into yawning and obstinate children."

When Emily returned home in 1839, it was Anne's turn to depart, going to work as a governess. In May, Charlotte went to a similar post. Governesses were in demand among the newly rich manufacturing families of the region. Neither Anne nor Charlotte liked the work, "wearily toiling to impart knowledge into yawning and obstinate children," interspersed with "reams of needlework." In *Shirley*, a governess protests against such a life:

It was in no sort concealed from me that I was held a "burden and restraint in society." The gentlemen I found regarded me as a "tabooed woman." The ladies too made it plain that they thought me "a bore." The servants detested me . . . My life in this house was sedentary, solitary, constrained, toilsome . . .

(Charlotte, *Shirley*, Chapter 21, 1849)

Anne Brontë, drawn by Charlotte. It has been suggested that Anne was secretly in love with her father's curate, William Weightman, who died of cholera in 1842.

If Emily's diary paper of 1841 speaks of the family "dragging on," there were good times, too. Patrick's new curate, William Weightman, charmed all the family. He was handsome, lively and clever, and shocked the girls by sending them Valentines. For Anne, it was, perhaps, more than friendship, a secret love cruelly ended by Weightman's early death from cholera in 1842.

> Yes, thou art gone! and never more
> Thy sunny smile shall gladden me;
> But I may pass the old church door,
> And pace the floor that covers thee,
>
> May stand upon the cold, damp stone,
> And think that, frozen, lies below
> The lightest heart that I have known,
> The kindest I shall ever know.
>
> (Anne, April 1844)

Opposite Emily worked hard at the Pensionnat Heger in Brussels, making remarkable progress in languages and music. She was also a talented artist. She gave this drawing of a broken pine tree to a Brussels friend, one of the few people she liked outside her family.

In the late 1830s, Charlotte's writing moved into a new maturity. Her sequence of Angrian novelettes – *Mina Laury* (1838), *Henry Hastings* and *Caroline Vernon* (1839) – ended with a "farewell to Angria":

I long to quit a while that burning clime where we have sojourned too long – its skies aflame – the glow of sunset is always upon it – the mind would cease from excitement and turn now to a cooler region where the dawn breaks grey and sober . . .

(Charlotte, late 1839)

Another stage in her literary apprenticeship now followed with "many a crude effort, destroyed almost as soon as composed." Angrian characters were now transferred to English settings. The literary critic, Christine Alexander, has studied all the early works and has noted how certain motifs and themes – the search for love, the unloved orphan, the lonely governess, the rival brothers – were to be revived and enlarged in the mature novels.

Emily's 1841 diary paper also mentions the sisters' new plan: to start a school of their own. Charlotte was advised that, to compete in the market, they must offer languages. She conceived a bold idea: they should go to study in Brussels, a city where her friend Mary Taylor had recently lived and studied. Aunt Branwell agreed to lend Charlotte and Emily money for this purpose, and Patrick, who at first thought them "wild and ambitious," was won over. In February 1842, he personally escorted them to the Pensionnat Heger, their chosen school.

"I think we have done well – we have got a very good school – and are considerably comfortable," Charlotte wrote to Ellen. Madame Heger was the director, while her husband was a visiting teacher. Monsieur Heger did not at first impress Charlotte; she saw him as "a little black being with a face that varies in expression. Sometimes he borrows the lineaments of an insane tomcat, sometimes those of a delirious hyena." Yet this was the man with whom Charlotte was later to fall hopelessly in love.

Both sisters still suffered from "overpowering shyness," yet they struggled to make their stay a success. Emily "worked like a horse," making striking progress

*The Pensionnat
Heger, photographed
in the 1840s.
Charlotte and Emily
went to Belgium in
February 1842 to
study at the school.*

in French, German, and above all music, where she showed real talent. Monsieur Heger respected Charlotte, but he deeply admired Emily's brilliant, unconventional mind. He found it hard, however, to reconcile this admiration with the common view of women, which did not see them as intellectuals. "She should have been a man," he told Elizabeth Gaskell. "Her powerful reason would have produced new spheres of discovery from the knowledge of the old; and her strong imperious will would never have been daunted by opposition or difficulty; never would have given way but with life."

In November 1842, the sisters were called home by the sudden death of Aunt Branwell. The only young Brontë present at her deathbed was Branwell, at home again, having been dismissed from his job as a railroad clerk for his carelessness in keeping accounts.

The sisters intended to use the legacies from their aunt's will for their school. Charlotte returned to Brussels; Anne went back to her second governess post with the Robinson family at Thorp Green, near York, taking Branwell as tutor to the Robinsons' son; and Emily remained, where she was most happy, at home, mixing studies with her housekeeping: "It was Emily who made all the bread for the family," noted Elizabeth Gaskell, "and anyone passing by the kitchen door might have seen her studying German out of an open book, propped before her as she kneaded the dough."

Charlotte's pleasure at returning to Brussels soon faded. She was now a teacher, not a pupil, and the girls

After the death of Aunt Branwell, Emily was happy to stay at the Parsonage to keep house. This is the kitchen where she made all the bread for the family, studying her German books as she kneaded the dough: this display at the Brontë Museum has recreated the scene.

47

Mr Taylor est revenu, je lui ai demandé s'il n'avait
une lettre pour moi - "Non, rien." "Patience - dit
la sœur viendra bientôt." Mademoiselle Taylor
revenue "Je n'ai rien pour vous de la part de Mr
Heger" dit elle "ni lettre ni message."

Ayant bien compris ces mots - je me suis dit, ce
je dirais à un autre en pareille circonstance: "Il faut
résigner et, surtout, ne pas vous affliger d'un malheur
que vous n'avez pas mérité." Je me suis efforcée de
pas pleurer à ne pas me plaindre -

... quand on ne se plaint pas et qu'on veut
... les feuilles se révoltent et on pai...
calme extérieur d'une lutte intérieure presque insuff...

Jour et nuit je ne trouve ni repos ni paix - si
je fais des rêves tourmentants où je vous vois toujours
toujours sombre et irrité contre moi -

Pardonnez-moi donc Monsieur si je prends la partie
vous écrire encore - Comment puis je supporter la v...

were awkward and rebellious. Madame Heger perceived Charlotte's unexpressed passion for her husband and stopped their private English lessons together. Charlotte drifted into loneliness and unhappiness, a "Robinson Crusoe-like condition," described in a letter to Ellen:

> One day is like another in this place . . . It sometimes happens that I am left, during several hours, quite alone, with four great desolate schoolrooms at my disposition. I try to read, I try to write, but in vain. I then wander from room to room, but the silence and loneliness of all the house weighs one's spirits like lead.

> (Charlotte, letter to Ellen, November 15, 1843)

Only when she gave up her post and returned to England in January 1844, did Charlotte understand and admit her passion for Monsieur Heger. For two years she suffered in secret, sending letter after letter to "my dear master."

> Day and night I find neither rest nor peace. If I sleep, I am disturbed by tormenting dreams in which I see you, always severe, always grave, always incensed against me . . . If my master withdraws his friendship from me entirely I shall be altogether without hope . . .

> (Charlotte, letter to M. Heger, January 8, 1845)

She endured torments as she waited for the mail: "When day by day I await a letter, and when day by day disappointment must come . . . I lose appetite and sleep – I pine away." But there were no answers. Monsieur Heger tore up her letters; watchful Madame Heger retrieved the pieces and sewed them together to read what Charlotte said.

Life for all the Brontës was made worse, in 1845, by Branwell's decline. He had been accused by Mr. Robinson of conducting a love affair with his wife, and dismissed. He collapsed into a mixture of despair, self-pity and drunkenness. "We have had sad work with Branwell," wrote Charlotte to Ellen. "He thought of nothing but stunning and drowning his distress of mind. No one in the house could rest." Even Emily now saw him as "a hopeless being."

The school project had also died. Prospectuses had been printed and circulated, but there were no replies.

Opposite One of Charlotte's passionate love letters to Monsieur Heger, her teacher in Brussels. He tore the letters up, but his wife retrieved the pieces and sewed them together so that she could read them. The stitches can be clearly seen.

"It was found no go," wrote Emily in her diary note of 1845. It was at this grim time that a new idea suddenly changed the sisters' prospects.

The Misses Bronte's Establishment

FOR

THE BOARD AND EDUCATION

OF A LIMITED NUMBER OF

YOUNG LADIES,

THE PARSONAGE, HAWORTH,

NEAR BRADFORD.

Terms.

	£.	s.	d.
BOARD AND EDUCATION, including Writing, Arithmetic, History, Grammar, Geography, and Needle Work, per Annum, ...	35	0	0
French, German, Latin } .. .. each per Quarter, ...	1	1	0
Music, Drawing,.. } .. .. each per Quarter, ...	1	1	0
Use of Piano Forte, per Quarter, ...	0	5	0
Washing, per Quarter, ...	0	15	0

Each Young Lady to be provided with One Pair of Sheets, Pillow Cases, Four Towels, a Dessert and Tea-spoon.

A Quarter's Notice, or a Quarter's Board, is required previous to the Removal of a Pupil.

4 The Dream of Becoming Authors

"The Gondals still flourish as bright as ever," noted Emily in the 1845 diary paper. "We intend sticking firmly by the rascals as long as they delight us." Anne's note also mentions Gondal, but she wonders about Emily's other writing, kept secret even from her: "She is writing some poetry too. I wonder what it is about?"

Emily's diary paper of July 1845. She is seen in her bedroom with her portable writing desk on her knee, and her beloved dog Keeper beside her.

In her sisters' absence, Emily had divided her poetry into two categories – personal and Gondal – and had transcribed them into two notebooks, kept carefully locked in her portable writing desk. One day, probably in October 1845, she left her Gondal notebook on this desk, where Charlotte found it and began to read.

> Something more than surprise seized me – a deep conviction that these were not common effusions, nor at all like the poetry women generally write. I thought them condensed and terse, vigorous and genuine. To my ear, they also had a peculiar music – wild, melancholy and elevating.
>
> (Charlotte, *Ellis Bell, biographical notice*, 1850)

When Emily's anger at this invasion of her cherished privacy had subsided, Charlotte persuaded her sisters to attempt a joint publication of their poems.

> We had very early cherished the dream of one day becoming authors. This dream . . . now suddenly acquired strength and consistency: it took the character

The pen-name signatures of the Brontë sisters: Currer (Charlotte); Ellis (Emily) and Acton (Anne) Bell. The masculine names, which kept their real initials, were used to avoid publishers' prejudice against women writers.

of a resolve. We agreed to arrange a small selection of
our poetry, and, if possible, get them published.

(Charlotte, *Ellis Bell, biographical notice*, 1850)

Emily insisted on their assuming pen-names before she
agreed to the project. This they did, choosing Currer
(Charlotte), Ellis (Emily) and Acton (Anne) Bell, avoiding
names that were obviously masculine, but feeling also
that "authoresses are liable to be looked upon with prejudice." They retained their own initials, and took "Bell"
from their father's new curate, Arthur Bell Nicholls.

The business-like Charlotte approached publishers.
In 1846, Aylott and Jones, a London firm, agreed to
produce the poems if the sisters contributed to the costs.
In May, *Poems*, by Currer, Ellis and Acton Bell, was
published. It was a failure; only two copies were sold.
"No man needs it or heeds it," wrote Charlotte sadly.

One sharp reviewer, however, chose Emily as the poet
with real talent. Ellis Bell had "an inspiration, which
may yet find an audience in the outer world . . . an
evident power of wing that may reach heights not here
attempted." Twenty-one of Emily's poems appeared in
the collection. In all, she wrote about 200, most of which
were not published until many years after her death.
Her simple verse forms recall Sir Walter Scott. Her plain
diction may have been influenced by the theories and
example of Wordsworth. The spirit and content of her
verse seems to resemble Shelley, whom she had probably read, and, coincidentally, Blake, whom she had
not. The force of her apparently simple verse is shown
in one of the best of the Gondal elegies, striking for its
bold repetitions:

Cold in the earth, and the deep snow piled above thee!
Far, far removed, cold in the dreary grave!
Have I forgot, my only love, to love thee,
Severed at last by Time's all-wearing wave? . . .

No other sun has lightened up my heaven;
No other star has ever shone for me:
All my life's bliss from thy dear life was given –
All my life's bliss is in the grave with thee.

(Emily, from *R. Alcona to J. Brenzaida*, March 3, 1845)

Charlotte observed her sister's capacity for visionary meditation, and ascribed this gift to her character, Shirley, in the novel of 1849:

> A still deep inborn delight glows in her – the pure gift of God to his creature . . . Buoyant, by green steps, by glad hills, all verdure and light, she reaches a station scarcely lower than that whence angels look down.

> (Charlotte, *Shirley*, Chapter 22, 1849)

Emily's poem "Silent is the house" is one of her mystical meditations, in which she offers her "vision" embedded in a Gondal story. Rochelle, a beautiful Gondal princess, is in prison, saved from despair only by a mysterious "wanderer," a "messenger of hope" who:

> . . . comes every night to me
> And offers for short life, eternal liberty.
>
> He comes with western winds, with evening's
>   wandering airs,
> With that clear dusk of heaven that brings the thickest
>   stars;
> Winds take a pensive tone, and stars a tender fire;
> And visions rise and change which kill me with desire –
>
> But first a hush of peace, a soundless calm descends;
> The struggle of distress and fierce impatience ends;
> Mute music soothes my breast – unuttered harmony
> That I could never dream till earth was lost to me.
>
> Then dawns the Invisible, the Unseen its truth reveals;
> My outward sense is gone, my inward essence feels –
> Its wings are almost free, its home, its harbour found;
> Measuring the gulf it stoops and dares the final bound!

(Emily, from *Julian M. and A.G. Rochelle*, October 9, 1845)

It would be too easy to see the vision simply as God or Christ. Emily was impatient with the confines of conventional religion. Her God has been defined as "a creedless immortal energy . . . this sense of infinity and immortality." This concept resembles Wordsworth's feeling of unity with a gigantic divine force within the universe:

Whose dwelling is the light of setting suns,
And the round ocean and the living air.
. . . A motion and a spirit, that impels
All thinking things, all objects of all thought,
And rolls through all things.

(William Wordsworth, *Tintern Abbey*, 1798)

Although the 1846 poetry collection was a failure, Charlotte noted that "the mere effort to succeed had given a wonderful zest to existence. It must be pursued." During the spring of 1846, each sister was hard at work on a novel: Charlotte on *The Professor*, Anne on *Agnes Grey* and Emily on *Wuthering Heights*.

It was a golden period of intense creativity. When their father had retired to bed, the girls were free, as was their custom, to walk around and around the dining room, pacing "like restless wild animals" as they discussed their work. They read passages aloud, criticized each other, gave suggestions.

Opposite *Emily by Branwell. An early reviewer of the sisters' work recognized Emily as a talented visionary poet.*

William Wordsworth was another poet admired by all the Brontës. His "pantheism" – seeing the divine in nature – was an experience that Emily shared.

The dining room at Haworth Parsonage. The sisters wrote at this table (one of their writing cases and a quill pen can be seen on it). They used to walk around the room "like restless wild animals," as they discussed their work. Emily died on the black sofa against the far wall.

When their "three distinct and unconnected tales" were finished, they were sent off to various publishers, but all three were repeatedly rejected. This was a dark hour. The rejected manuscript of *The Professor* was returned to Charlotte on the very morning that she stood at the side of her elderly father as he underwent a painful eye operation. Nevertheless, at this time of crisis, the "brave genius" Charlotte began writing *Jane Eyre*, the novel that was to transform her life. She wrote as if inspired, as she later told Elizabeth Gaskell: "The progress of her tale lay clear and bright before her, in distinct vision."

In July 1847 a new publisher, T.C. Newby, offered to publish *Agnes Grey* and *Wuthering Heights*, if the authors assisted with the costs. He did not want *The Professor*, and nor did Smith Elder and Company, but they at least expressed interest in any future novel Currer Bell might produce. Charlotte hastened to finish her second book and on August 24 told the publisher, "I now send you per rail a MS entitled *Jane Eyre*, a novel in three volumes by Currer Bell."

The first page of the manuscript of Jane Eyre. *Charlotte began writing it in August 1846, a very dark time in her life.*

Jane Eyre
by Currer Bell

Vol. I.

Chap. 1st.

There was no possibility of taking a walk that day. We had been wandering indeed in the leafless shrubbery an hour in the morning, but since dinner (Mrs. Reed, when there was no company, dined early) the cold winter wind had brought with it clouds so sombre, a rain so penetrating that further out-door exercise was now out of the question.

I was glad of it; I never liked long walks especially on chilly afternoons; dreadful to me was the coming home in the raw twilight with nipped fingers and toes and a heart saddened by the chidings of Bessie, the nurse, and humbled by the consciousness of my physical inferiority to Eliza, John and Georgiana Reed.

George Smith, the firm's head, and his reader, W.S.
Williams, were the first to taste the book's absorbing
power. Smith began reading on a Sunday morning,
became fascinated, lunched off a sandwich, read on,
rushed through dinner and finished the book late at
night. *Jane Eyre* was accepted the next day and published
on October 16, 1847.

The readers' excitement was soon echoed in reviews
and journals. William Thackeray, the already famous
novelist, wrote:

> . . . I have lost (or won, if you like) a whole day in
> reading it . . . It is a fine book through – the man and
> woman capital – some of her love passages made me
> cry – to the astonishment of John who came in with the
> coals – I have been exceedingly moved and pleased.

(William Thackeray, letter, October 28, 1847)

The quiet author plucked up courage to show a copy
of the book to her father. "When he came in to tea,"
she told Elizabeth Gaskell, "he said, 'Girls, do you know
that Charlotte has been writing a book, and it is much
better than likely.'"

Jane Eyre sold well, and this stimulated the sluggish
T.C. Newby into action. In December 1847, *Wuthering
Heights* and *Agnes Grey* were also published. The sisters'
old "dream of becoming authors" had now become a
reality.

The novels of the Brontë sisters are very much rooted
in the social conditions and the literary traditions of their
time. They show the influence of the romantic writers
of the preceding half-century, especially Scott,
Wordsworth, Shelley and Byron. However, the sisters
also developed the established form of the nineteenth-
century novel in a number of ways, bringing in a more
sophisticated view of the psychological lives of characters, as well as new ways of telling a story. They also
involve questions of social class, religion and morality,
and important issues of the time such as industrialization
and colonialism.

Jane Eyre is the story of an orphan governess, "plain,
poor and little," who falls in love with her employer,
Mr. Rochester of Thornfield Hall. The story, told by Jane

Thornfield Hall, where Jane Eyre goes to work as a governess for the mysterious Mr. Rochester. Charlotte based the Hall on various Yorkshire mansions that she had visited.

herself, moves from her unhappiness and feelings of physical and social inferiority, through many painful twists of fortune, to her fulfillment in a marriage of "equals."

As a tale of personal growth, the novel is in the tradition of the romantic literature of the late eighteenth and early nineteenth centuries. Rochester, who developed from the Zamornas of Charlotte's early writing, is in many ways like one of Byron's heroes: dark, craggy-browed, athletic and mysterious. Some elements of the novel recall the "Gothic" novels – chilling tales of fantasy and horror – that were popular at the time. Thornfield Hall suggests the mysterious houses of Gothic fiction, in which the heroine's sensibility is tried, her strength proved and her self-knowledge enhanced. Mrs. Rochester, the "madwoman in the attic" at Thornfield, echoes the same tradition, in which ghosts or lunatics point to the supernatural or irrational.

However, although she freely used the audience's familiarity with popular fiction in this way, Charlotte aimed to produce a fiction "real, cool and solid," which would be true to the complexities of human psychology, as well as precise in factual detail. All the mysterious and frightening aspects of the story are eventually explained by reason and fact, to form part of the development of Jane's character, and of the novel's critical view of the society of the day. Mrs. Rochester is not a ghost, but is part of a tale of human sorrow, greed, deception and social ambition. Mr. Rochester may look like a Byronic hero, but his gloom can be explained by the facts of lingering misfortune. His disfigurement at the end of the novel abruptly ends the reader's expectations of a popular romantic hero.

Charlotte tells a good story in *Jane Eyre*. Dramatic episodes create suspense: Jane's hearing the mad woman's laugh, "distinct, formal, mirthless," in the upper story of Thornfield Hall; the breaking off of Jane's wedding to Rochester when a voice in the church cries, "The marriage cannot go on: I declare the existence of an impediment"; Jane's shock at returning to Thornfield Hall to find it destroyed by fire.

Symbolic elements add meaning to Jane's story. In the claustrophobic Gateshead, Jane experiences the extremes of fiery (red) passion and cold (white) repression, which become opposite elements in her journey; dangers both outside and within her. They reoccur and develop at the unhealthily cold Lowood School, during the moral tests of Thornfield, and at Moor House where she is tempted to deny her deepest feelings and to marry St. John Rivers, only to be resolved in the peace of Ferndean.

Jane's progress to maturity and independence of mind involves pushing aside the various nineteenth-century female roles that are pressed upon her. At Lowood she gazes at:

> . . . the hilly horizons: My eye passed all other objects to rest on those most remote, the blue peaks. It was those I longed to surmount . . . I desired liberty; for liberty I gasped; for liberty I uttered a prayer.

However, it is only when Jane has fully established

Places have great symbolic importance in Jane Eyre. *At Gateshead Hall, where Jane lives as a child, she experiences the extremes of passion and repression that recur throughout her story.*

Opposite *Rochester is blinded and mutilated in the fire at Thornfield.*

her own identity that she is ready to meet Rochester as an equal. Both refer to the mysterious bond between them, but Jane insists on the equality of their union:

> It is my spirit that addresses your spirit, just as if both had passed through the grave, and we stood at God's feet equal – as we are!

This equality, though, is threatened by the social prejudice and legal constraints of the age, and can be fulfilled only in the natural setting of Ferndean, away from the social world. In this way, Charlotte presents a recurring theme of her, and her sisters', work: the status of women, and their financial dependency on men, whether as children, wives, mistresses or governesses.

When Rochester insists that Jane will "give up your governessing slavery" upon marrying, Jane warns that she will not exchange this role for that of an expensively decorated, but inferior wife. Instead, she says, "I'll . . . go out as a missionary to preach liberty to them that are enslaved."

Jane achieves this equality not only with Rochester but also with St. John Rivers, once she realizes that he is not the saint he seemed; and this recognition saves her from the loveless marriage he proposes:

> I was with an equal – one with whom I might argue – one whom, if I saw good, I might resist.

Having realized her equality with the men around her, Jane has the right to act independently, and to protect the life of her feelings. This is the "liberty" she has longed for. This freedom of choice is reflected in the novel's most quoted line, in which Jane addresses the reader directly:

> Reader, I married him.

Jane, as the author of her story, is now also the author of her own life and happiness.

Wuthering Heights is a tightly structured novel, using several narrators to unfold a tale of extraordinary experience and great emotional power. Its first reviewers did not quite know what to make of it, calling it "a strange sort of book – baffling all regular criticism." Complaints against "coarseness" (which meant variously expressions of religious impropriety, or even criticism of the lives of the wealthy) had been raised already against *Jane Eyre*. Now they became a chorus. "The reader is shocked, disgusted, almost sickened by details of cruelty, inhumanity, and the most diabolical hate of vengeance," wrote one reviewer.

There were, however, gleams of encouragement in some fairly favorable reviews that Emily kept in her writing desk. One saw a "rugged power," which showed that "the work of Ellis Bell is only a promise but it is a colossal one." Charlotte came to the book's defense in her 1850 preface, likening its central idea to "a granite block on a solitary moor" which Ellis Bell had "wrought with a rude chisel, and from no model, but the vision

of his meditations." By this time, the critical tide was turning, and by the end of the century, key essays by Swinburne and, in 1900, by Mrs. Humphrey Ward, established Emily above Charlotte, and most other Victorian novelists, as showing "the many-sidedness to which only the great attain."

The major part of the narrative is told by Ellen Dean (Nelly), a lifelong servant at Wuthering Heights, the old house on the moors. Nelly tells in straightforward fashion the tale of Catherine and Heathcliff's unearthly passion and his cruel revenge, locating these extraordinary events within the familiar detail of everyday life. She recounts, for the amusement of the convalescent visitor, Lockwood, the history of the Earnshaw family at the Heights, and the Lintons from the milder, more peaceful Thrushcross Grange, from the time that old Mr. Earnshaw brings home the orphan Heathcliff, "a little black-haired swarthy thing so dark as if it came from the devil." So Lockwood, and the reader, learn of the childhood attachment of Heathcliff and Earnshaw's daughter Catherine, of Catherine's marriage to Edgar Linton and her subsequent death, and Heathcliff's prolonged and cruel revenge on both families. A succeeding generation defies Heathcliff's project, for when Catherine's daughter Cathy Linton and the deprived heir Hareton Earnshaw fall in love, natural affection and family possession are restored to Wuthering Heights.

This is a novel of great contrasts in its narrative, action, settings and imagery: between the rough Heights and the gentle Grange; the wild and the civilized; earth and heaven; body and soul; warmth and cold; male and female; discord and harmony; good and evil. However, Emily Brontë's novel displays a strong urge to see beyond these simple oppositions. Thus it portrays the struggle toward an impossible but ideal union between two opposites.

Catherine and Heathcliff's passion has about it the intensity of desire that characterized the yearning in Emily Brontë's poems for freedom of soul. In their childhood, Catherine and Heathcliff develop a relationship that is almost shared being. Catherine protests: "I am Heathcliff." However, growing out of childhood means becoming aware of the oppositions cherished by society: of male and female, rich and poor, cultivated and

Opposite *The opening of* Wuthering Heights, *where Lockwood, tenant of Thrushcross Grange, visits his landlord, Heathcliff, at the hill farm. In describing Wuthering Heights, Emily may have borrowed certain features – like the carving over the doorway – from High Sunderland House near Halifax.*

uncouth. The novel shows how society's demands for separateness bring with them an intolerable sense of loss and desire for reunion.

The bond between Catherine and Heathcliff seems to go beyond the physical and even, it is implied, beyond life itself. Catherine says that Heathcliff is "more myself

Wuthering Heights in its dramatic moorland setting.

Cathy and Heathcliff as children in a film version of the novel.

than I am. Whatever our souls are made of, his and mine are the same."

Both are frustrated, however, by the knowledge that the spirit they yearn for is encased in the physical body and daily existence of the other. Catherine's bodily frailty becomes an enemy to Heathcliff, as it leads to her early death; but as they are separated, his own strength also becomes an evil: "So much the worse for me that I am strong. Do I want to live?"

There are many references to heaven and hell in relation to Catherine and Heathcliff, but conventional ideas of an afterlife only serve as a contrast to their story: the heaven they seek is union, and hell is separation. Catherine dreams that she is an alien in heaven:

> The angels were so angry that they flung me out, into the middle of the heath on top of Wuthering Heights, where I woke sobbing for joy.

However, when she is married to Edgar Linton, starved of the love she needs and threatened by her physical weakness, Catherine turns from earthly life as from a betrayer:

> I shall love [my Heathcliff] yet; and take him with me: he's in my soul. And the thing that irks me most is this shattered prism after all.

For Heathcliff, Catherine's escape from earthly life is his own personal hell:

> Where is she? Not there – not in heaven – not perished – Where? . . . Be with me always – take any form – drive me mad! Only do not leave me in this abyss, where I cannot find you!

However, his own heaven comes in sight when his bodily strength, which had prevented him from reaching the "one universal idea," begins to fail. Now Heathcliff assumes a strange look of joy, "wild and glad" – echoing terms elsewhere associated with an active heaven in the novel. The fact that the hated separation is coming to an end is suggested by the symbolic coming together of opposites. Nelly says that Heathcliff's "raptured expression" suggests "both pleasure and pain, in exquisite

Opposite *The marriage of Cathy and Edgar Linton embitters Heathcliff and inspires him to a long and ferocious revenge against the Earnshaws and the Lintons.*

extremes"; and Heathcliff explains his own paradoxical happiness: "I'm too happy, and yet not happy enough. My soul's bliss kills my body, but does not satisfy itself."

Charlotte Brontë described her sister's book as though it were sculpted from nature, from the "granite block on a solitary moor." Nature in *Wuthering Heights* is represented by the powerful and beautiful setting of the North Yorkshire moors, and has its own significance. The moors around the Heights change their mood: always wild, they can also be hostile or comforting, exhausting or invigorating, according to the weather and the observer's disposition. Nature, then, includes all the opposites that are separated in the social world, and points to a fullness of life that society excludes.

The novel's characters are often described through natural imagery. Nelly introduces the contrast between Edgar Linton and Heathcliff by associating each with the landscape: "The contrast resembled what you see in exchanging a bleak, hilly coal country for a beautiful fertile valley." Catherine's life is closely linked to nature. She fades through an autumn, and winter comes with her death: "The day she was buried came a fall of snow . . . It blew bleak as winter." Even after death she is a ghostly presence in nature, and Heathcliff finds his love of her, 'in every cloud, in every tree."

Heathcliff can be seen to represent a wild and terrifying side of nature: no one knows his human origins, and he has no humane sensibilities. Like nature itself, Heathcliff can be cruel and irrationally harsh; nevertheless, the reader can sympathize with his desire for reunion with Catherine.

Wuthering Heights has a circular structure. Lockwood's narrative, and with it Nelly's, circle back to the book's starting point as another new spring returns after many bleak winters. The central action of the book is thus completed, but not explained; order and harmony seem restored, but we do not know the fate of the unsatisfied passions of the story. The fate beyond death of the love of Catherine and Heathcliff remains a mystery: no one knows whether they are at last united. Ghosts may or may not walk the moors. The story-tellers know no more and fall silent, as the mood of nature returns to quietness, and Lockwood contemplates the graves of Catherine, Edgar and Heathcliff:

I lingered round them, under that benign sky; watched the moths, fluttering among the heath and harebells; listened to the soft wind breathing through the grass; and wondered how anyone could ever imagine unquiet slumbers for the sleepers in that quiet earth.'

(Emily, *Wuthering Heights*, Ch. 34, 1847)

Anne's *Agnes Grey* is a very different novel, a simple first-person narrative that describes the difficult life of a governess, Agnes, who longs to be independent:

To go out into the world, to enter upon a new life; to act for myself; to exercise my unused faculties; to try my unknown powers; to earn my own maintenance, and something to comfort and help my father, mother and sister . . .

(Anne, *Agnes Grey*, Ch. 1)

Opposite *The passion of Cathy and Heathcliff dominates the novel: a still from the 1973 film.*

Richard Redgrave's "The Governess" perfectly illustrates the miserable life of these young women, as experienced by Agnes Grey. The sad young governess contrasts with her spoiled and carefree girl charges.

Opposite *Anne's*
The Tenant of
Wildfell Hall *warned
against the dangers of
alcohol. Heavy
drinking helped to kill
Branwell, who died in
1848.*

However, as governess to two wealthy families, Agnes finds that rather than gaining the independence she had longed for, she is exploited, her moral instincts are offended, and her emotional life unfulfilled. The callousness of the upper classes and their disrespect for education are sharply criticized throughout the novel: at one point Agnes is forced to drop a large stone on a nest of baby birds before they are tortured to death by the son of the family. The second family is just as bad, and Agnes begins to feel that her work is futile. She receives the mother's instructions:

> For the girls she seemed anxious only to render them as superficially attractive and showily accomplished as they could possibly be made, without present trouble or discomfort to themselves . . . With regard to the two boys, it was much the same . . . I was to get the greatest possible quantity of Latin grammar into their heads, in order to fit them for school without trouble to themselves.
>
> (Anne, *Agnes Grey*, Ch. 7)

Only after much suffering does Agnes find happiness in her marriage with the curate Mr. Weston.

Anne's second novel, *The Tenant of Wildfell Hall*, published in June 1848, showed her determination and deep compassion. Into it she poured all her wretchedness at watching the decline of the dissolute Branwell. "She brooded over it till she believed it to be a duty to reproduce every detail as a warning to others," wrote Charlotte. An early critic accused her of "a morbid love of the coarse, if not the brutal" in her study of the deterioration of the drunkard, Arthur Huntingdon, and the trials of Helen, his wife. Anne replied forcefully:

> Is it better to reveal the snares and pitfalls of life to the young and thoughtless traveller, or to cover them with branches and flowers? . . . If there were less of this delicate concealment of facts . . . there would be less of sin and misery to the young of both sexes who are left to wring their bitter knowledge from experience . . .
>
> (Anne, Preface to *The Tenant of Wildfell Hall*, 1848)

THE TENANT

OF

WILDFELL HALL.

BY

ANNE BRONTË.

On the Moors.

LONDON :

SMITH, ELDER AND CO., 15 WATERLOO PLACE.

1873.

The Tenant of Wildfell Hall is a sophisticated narrative, containing some powerful scenes. Helen Huntingdon's diary tells her story within the framework of Gilbert Markham's letters to his brother-in-law. These methods lend a documentary authenticity to the tale, while flashbacks, interruptions and information withheld contribute drama and suspense.

The material of Anne's novel is striking: Helen's leaving her husband to save their son from corruption was, by the standards of the time, a desperate – even immoral – act. May Sinclair, writing sixty years later, could still sense the shock of the gesture: "The slamming of Helen Huntingdon's bedroom door against her husband reverberated throughout Victorian England."

Huntingdon's deathbed scene is also memorable for its shocking power:

Nothing could comfort him now – the world was nothing to him: life and all its interests, its petty cares and transient pleasures, were a cruel mockery. To talk of the past was to torture him with vain remorse; to refer to the future was to increase his anguish . . . Often he dwelt with shuddering minuteness on the fate of his perishing clay – the slow, piecemeal dissolution already invading his frame; the shroud, the coffin, the dark, lonely grave, and all the horrors of corruption.

(Anne, *The Tenant of Wildfell Hall*, Ch. 49)

Helen's strength in attending her dying husband balances her courage in removing herself from him. Only when Markham fully understands that she has shown great moral courage, can he appropriately realize his love for Helen.

An engraving of Wildfell Hall. The beautiful Helen Huntingdon, who calls herself Mrs. Graham after her elopement, is its mysterious tenant.

5 Shocks, Sufferings, Losses

1848, which was to be a year of disaster for the Brontës, began auspiciously enough. A third edition of *Jane Eyre* appeared, as conjecture about the true identity of Currer Bell, "this great, unknown genius" and "his" brothers ran through literary London. "The common rumour is that they are brothers of the weaving order in some Lancashire town," noted an editor. The mystery began to be inconvenient when the unscrupulous Newby published *The Tenant of Wildfell Hall*, suggesting in his advertising that it, too, was by the best-selling author, Currer Bell. When a puzzled letter from Smith Elder reached Charlotte, she and Anne decided to "whirl up by the night train" to London to reveal their identities to the publisher.

George Smith's later description of his first meeting with the "Bells" reveals some of the prevailing attitudes toward women that the sisters had sought to avoid by writing under pseudonyms:

> I was at work in my room when a clerk reported that two ladies wished to see me . . . Two rather quaintly-dressed little ladies, pale-faced and anxious looking, walked into my room; one of them came forward and presented me with a letter addressed, in my own handwriting, to "Currer Bell Esq." I noticed the letter had been opened, and said, with some sharpness: "Where did you get this from?" "From the post office," was the reply. "It was addressed to me. We have both come that you might have ocular proof there are at least two of us." This, then, was "Currer Bell" in person.

(George Smith, *The Critic*, 1901)

A photograph of George Smith, the publisher who was quick to see the power of Jane Eyre, *which he produced in 1847. Circumstances forced Charlotte to reveal the true identities of the Bells, when she visited Smith in London in 1848.*

Smith made hasty plans to entertain the new literary stars, and had time to study them. His remarks attempt to place the writers in relation to the age's view of femininity, drawing attention toward their appearance and away from their work. In Anne he saw "a wish for protection and encouragement . . . a kind of constant appeal, which invited sympathy . . . She was by no means pretty, yet of a pleasing appearance." Charlotte,

he noted, was "interesting rather than attractive. She
was very small and had a quaint old-fashioned look . . .
There was but little feminine charm about her; and of
this fact she was herself uneasily and perpetually con-
scious. . . ." He even assumed that "she would have
given all her genius and all her fame to have been beautiful." By revealing their identity, the sisters had lain
themselves open to such comments and speculation.
Yet there were compensations: in writing to Smith and
Williams, who became her valued advisers, Charlotte
was at last able to use her own name.

Branwell, at this time, was sinking into drunkenness
and opium addiction. He had been drinking heavily
since he was dismissed from his post as tutor at
Thorp Green in 1845. Tuberculosis took hold of
him, and on September 24, he died. Charlotte's
response was to the waste of a life that had seemed
so promising:

> I do not weep from a sense of bereavement – but for the
> wreck of talent, the ruin of promise, the untimely dreary
> extinction of what might have been a burning and
> shining light . . . Nothing remains of him but a memory
> of errors and suffering.

(Charlotte, letter to W.S. Williams, October 2, 1848)

A more dreadful loss now followed. Emily apparently
caught cold at Branwell's funeral, and the tuberculosis,
which, Charlotte later realized, had affected her for some
time, now began to destroy her with terrible speed. "She
made haste to leave us," Charlotte wrote bitterly. Her
fiercely individual character refused all help from
"poisoning doctors," as she called them, and she continued her ordinary routines, even tottering out, with
an apron full of scraps, to feed her beloved dogs. Her
sister watched her with admiration: "I have never seen
her parallel in anything. Stronger than a man, simpler
than a child, her nature stood alone."

On her last morning, December 19, Charlotte brought
her a sprig of heather from the moors, but Emily's "dim
and indifferent eyes" could no longer recognize it. Some-
how she dressed and went to the dining room to sew.
There, at two o'clock, lying on the black horsehair sofa,
she died. Her dog Keeper howled outside her bedroom
door for many days.

Jack Shaw, the Guardsman, and
Jack painter of Norfolk.

Question — "The half minute time's up, so
come to the ~~dead~~ scratch; wont you?"

Answer — "Blast your eyes, it's no use, for
I cannot come!"

A PARODY.

Emily's favorite dog, Keeper, drawn by her in 1838. When she died in December 1848, Keeper is said to have howled outside her door for many days.

Some sad comfort I take, as I hear the wind blow and feel the cutting keenness of the frost in knowing that the elements bring her no more suffering – their severity cannot reach her grave – her fever is quieted, her restlessness soothed, her deep, hollow cough is hushed for ever; we do not hear it in the night nor listen for it in the morning; we have not the conflict of the strangely strong spirit and the fragile frame before us – relentless conflict – once seen, never to be forgotten.

(Charlotte, letter to W.S. Williams, December 25, 1848)

Charlotte remained haunted by Emily's death. She was "as dear to me as life." She recalled bitterly how she "turned her dying eyes reluctantly from the pleasant sun," and the way that she was "rooted up in the prime of her days in the promise of her powers . . . her existence now lies, like a field of green corn trodden down, like a tree in full bearing struck at the root."

86

In January 1849, Anne, too, was diagnosed as tubercular. She bravely endured the crude, painful treatment of the time. "When we lost Emily I thought he had drained the very dregs of our cup of trial," Charlotte told Williams, "but now when I hear Anne cough as Emily coughed, I tremble lest there should be more exquisite bitterness yet to taste."

In May, the sisters and Ellen traveled to Scarborough, which Anne loved. "A peaceful sun gilded her evening," and there, on May 28, she died peacefully, and was buried in the seaside town. Charlotte could not conceal her despair: "Why life is so blank, brief and bitter I do not know."

Charlotte was deeply affected by Emily's early death: she was "as dear to me as life." This is one of Branwell's portraits of Emily.

Anne's drawing of a girl watching the sun set over the sea matches her sister's words about her death at Scarborough: "a peaceful sun gilded her evening."

When she eventually returned home, stunned by the "shocks, sufferings, losses" she had endured, she realized her new loneliness, especially when evening came and she went alone to the dining room where the sisters had so often talked, walked and written together.

I felt that the house was all silent – the rooms were all empty. I remembered where the three were laid – in what narrow, dark dwellings never more to reappear. So the sense of desolation and bitterness took possession of me.

(Charlotte, letter to Ellen, June 23, 1849)

Opposite *Anne was buried at St. Mary's Church, Scarborough, the Yorkshire seaside resort which she loved.*

6 Charlotte Alone

Charlotte found some relief from sorrow in the writing of her second novel, *Shirley*, published in October 1849. "The occupation of writing it has been a boon to me," she told Williams. "It took me out of dark and desolate reality into an unreal but happier region."

In *Shirley* Charlotte commented on aspects of the contemporary "condition of England" (a subject common to many Victorian writers) by looking back to the events of an earlier time: the Luddite riots in Yorkshire (1811–12), when unemployed weavers smashed the new mill machinery that had lost them their jobs. In this setting, a third-person narrative tells the twin love stories of Caroline Helstone and Shirley Keeldar. Charlotte's careful research into the period of the Napoleonic Wars, and the effects of mechanization on the Yorkshire wool trade, give substance to a study of women's needs and of social change.

In the novel, the frustrated violence of frame-breaking and food riots is linked to the frustrations of passivity and powerlessness that women experience. Through its two stories, of industrial strife and of love, with their many parallels and contrasts, the novel examines issues of equality and power, and makes a bold plea for change in the common view of marriage and women's roles:

Fathers . . . order them to stay at home. What do they expect them to do at home? If you ask, – they would answer, sew and cook. They expect them to do this, and this only, contentedly, regularly, uncomplainingly all

their lives long, as if they had no germs of faculties for anything else . . . Could men live so themselves? Would they not be very weary? . . . Would not their weariness ferment in time to frenzy? . . . Men of England! Look at your poor girls, many of them fading around you, dropping off into consumption or decline; or, what is worse, degenerating to sour old maids, – envious, backbiting, wretched, because life is a desert to them.

(Charlotte, *Shirley*, Ch. 22)

Haworth was now oppressive to Charlotte because of its memories, and she enjoyed several visits to London in the early 1850s. George Smith did his best to entertain her, although she was not an easy guest, with her earnestness and shyness. Some people were afraid of her, noted Smith, as she seemed to be "always engaged in observing and analyzing the people she met." She went to London Zoo and to the Great Exhibition of 1851, saw Turner's paintings, and watched Macready acting in a Shakespeare play. Everything was reported back to her father in letters, especially her seeing her childhood hero, the Duke of Wellington. Her identity was now widely known and she enjoyed considerable fame as an author. George Richmond's crayon portrait shows her at this time of success.

In August 1850 Charlotte made an important new friend, Elizabeth Gaskell, her future biographer and herself a well-known novelist. In a letter, Elizabeth Gaskell noted her first impressions of "a little lady in black silk gown . . . she is undeveloped; thin and more than half a head shorter than I . . . eyes (very good and expressive, looking straight at you) . . . large mouth and many teeth gone; altogether plain . . . She has a very sweet voice, rather hesitates in choosing her expressions, but when chosen they seem without an effort, admirable and just . . . She possesses a charming union of simplicity and power."

In 1853, she went to stay at Haworth, and enjoyed Charlotte's conversation, her "most original and suggestive thoughts" and the "wild strange facts of her own and her sisters' lives." She noticed how Charlotte still walked in the dining room as she and her sisters had always done: "She did come down every night, and begin the slow monotonous incessant walk in which I am sure I should fancy I heard the steps of the dead

following me. She says she could not sleep without it."

Illness delayed Charlotte's last complete novel, *Villette*, published in January 1853. A meeting in London with friends from her Brussels days turned her mind back to her experiences at the Pensionnat, which she had tried to use in *The Professor*. Now she possessed the detachment to turn the painful experience and her secret passion for Monsieur Heger into a striking narrative of a woman's need to fulfill and express herself.

As the story of an orphan and an outsider in a foreign city, *Villette* might seem related to romantic fiction; but like its heroine, the small, plain and apparently cold Lucy Snowe, it frequently denies the "spirit of romance." The novel tells of Lucy's solitary journey to find work in Villette (Brussels), at the school of the secretive, spying Madame Beck. It follows the heroine through her hopeless love for John Bretton, the young English doctor, and her long-resisted love for Paul Emmanuel, the unprepossessing but ultimately fascinating visiting teacher at the school, to her eventual independence. It is a study in loneliness, repression and loss, but also shows the need to respond to one's deepest feelings.

VILLETTE.

By CURRER BELL,

AUTHOR OF " JANE EYRE," " SHIRLEY," ETC.

IN THREE VOLUMES.

VOL. I.

LONDON:

SMITH, ELDER & CO., 65, CORNHILL.

SMITH, TAYLOR & CO., BOMBAY.

1853.

The Author of this work reserves the right of translating it.

Charlotte Brontë said of *Villette*: "Unless I am mistaken the emotion of the book will be found to be kept throughout in tolerable subjection." Yet, far from claiming that the book is without passion, this statement points to the presence of emotion kept under guard. Lucy Snowe is oppressed by her place in society: as an orphan she is confined to other people's houses, and as a single young woman she spends her time serving others in sickrooms, dormitories and classrooms. As a foreigner in Villette, her isolation and confinement are emphasized. She finds work in a school where all are subject to the surveillance of Madame Beck, which threatens Lucy's privacy and individuality. All these factors exert their pressure on Lucy's desire for security and fulfillment.

However, there is also a conflict within Lucy, between the part of her that feels, and longs for self-expression, and another that represses feelings and forms a protective shell around her to hide her true self. This has several effects. It protects her from the spying of Madame Beck, but it also makes her almost invisible to Dr. John, and prevents the sympathetic efforts of Monsieur Paul to read her character. The reader, however, is aware of both Lucy's surface image and her underlying self.

Lucy's attempts to suppress her feelings are reflected in the narrative, for she often says a thing, then seems to deny it, but without making it disappear for the reader. This trick is an extension of the way in which she claims to be cold, calm and detached, and assumes this manner in order to deceive those around her, yet at the same time lets us see that it is only a manner.

Lucy's narrative shows her journey through a life that often seems "a hopeless desert," but which is interrupted by storms symbolizing change or disaster. At times, however, happiness makes this life into a garden, charmed with "light breeze, fountain and foliage," as when Lucy is happy with Monsieur Paul. Now she discovers the nature and meaning of love, and that she should open herself to this happiness, even when no one can guarantee that it will last. At the end of *Villette*, Paul may or may not be drowned at sea, depending on the reader's interpretation. Now the storm imagery that has run throughout the novel can be seen as a

The garden in the Rue Fossette – the scene of some of the happier moments in Villette.

sign of change and loss, or as one of hope, as the reader chooses. Although we cannot be sure of what has happened, the novel recognizes the value of feelings and of self-acceptance, amid, and despite, the storms of change.

As Charlotte finished her last great love story, she entered a real love affair that gave her own life a poignant last twist. Arthur Bell Nicholls had been her father's hard-working and trusted curate since 1844. Now, at Christmas 1852, he suddenly came to Charlotte "shaking, from head to foot, looking deadly pale, speaking low," and declared his love for her. When Charlotte told her father, he flew into a temper, feeling that the match would degrade his now famous daughter and treated Nicholls with contempt. The curate found it hard to

disguise his distress, and sought another curacy in Yorkshire.

"I pity him inexpressibly," wrote Charlotte to Ellen. She allowed a secret correspondence to continue between them. She finally won her father round to accept Nicholls, and the couple were married in Haworth Church in June 1854, Patrick stolidly refusing to attend the service. The couple passed a happy honeymoon at the prosperous home of the Nicholls family in Ireland and then returned to live with Patrick at the Parsonage.

Patrick was the last survivor of the Brontë family.

Opposite *Arthur Bell Nicholls was appointed curate to Patrick Brontë in 1845. He married Charlotte in June 1854.*

Charlotte began another novel, *Emma*, left unfinished at her death as an intriguing fragment about a mysterious rich child abandoned by her father at a boarding school.

"Who are you?" demanded Miss Wilcox. "What do you know about yourself?"
A sort of half interjection escaped the girl's lips: it was a sound expressing partly fear, and partly the shock the nerves feel when an evil, very long expected, at last and suddenly arrives.

(Charlotte, *Emma*, Ch. 2, 1860)

Charlotte's married happiness was short lived. In pregnancy she became ill, and, after months of wasting sickness, died on March 31, 1855. Her last words were "We have been so happy."

*The memorial tablet to
the Brontë family in
Haworth Church.*

Ironically, her husband and father, who had been so at odds, were left together as grief-stricken survivors: "two," as Elizabeth Gaskell imagined them, "desolate and alone in the old grey house."

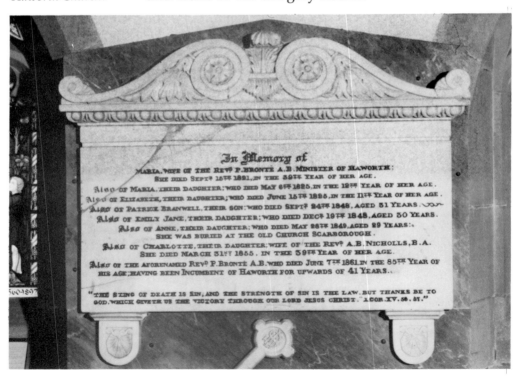

Elizabeth Gaskell's *Life of Charlotte Brontë*, published in 1857, was one memorial. The writer Charles Kingsley saw it in Victorian style as "a picture of a valiant woman made perfect by suffering." But Mary Taylor could only comment grimly: "People do not think it a strange or wrong state of things that a woman of first rate talents, industry and integrity should live all her life in a waking nightmare of poverty and self suppression."

Matthew Arnold's poem "Haworth Churchyard," published after Charlotte's death, was another memorial. Recalling the mood of the last paragraph of *Wuthering Heights*, he imagines the three sisters reunited in the grave:

> Sleep, O cluster of friends,
> Sleep! – or only when May
> Brought by the west wind, returns
> Back to your native heaths,
> And the plover is heard on the moors,
> Yearly awake to behold
> The opening summer, the sky,
> The shining moorland – to hear
> The drowsy bee, as of old,
> Hum o'er the thyme, the grouse
> Call from the heather in bloom!

> (Matthew Arnold, "Haworth Churchyard,"
> April 1855)

The Parsonage at Haworth as it is today. Every year it attracts thousands of visitors from all over the world, drawn there by the fascination of the Brontë story.

Glossary

Biography Someone's life story written by another person.

Curacy The office of a curate, the assistant to the vicar of a parish.

Diction A poet's choice and use of words.

Duke of Wellington Arthur Wellesley (1769–1852), the soldier and statesman whose compaigns led to the British victory in the Napoleonic Wars. The Brontë children read about him in *Blackwood's Magazine*.

Effusion An outpouring of emotion.

Elegy Writing about sadness and mourning.

Gothic Stories of fantasy and horror popular in the late eighteenth and early ninteenth centuries; Anne Radcliffe's *The Mysteries of Udolpho* (1791) is a famous example. *Jane Eyre* and *Villette* show Gothic influences; and both Emily and Charlotte mention "the foul German spectre – the Vampire," taken from Gothic tales translated from German in the 1830s.

Governess A woman employed in a private house to train and teach the children.

Headmaster A principal of a school.

Incumbency A religious office such as vicar of a parish.

Luddite Workers in the weaving trade in the north of England who protested, in the early nineteenth century, against the machines that were depriving them of work. The machine-breakers were named after one of their leaders, Ned Ludd.

Methodism The eighteenth-century religious movement led by John Wesley, which aimed to reform the sluggish Anglican Church by returning to the teachings of the Gospels.

Mystical Having divine or sacred meaning, beyond normal human understanding.

Narrative The telling of a story. First-person narrative is told by the person involved in the story, e.g. "*I* did this or that." Third-person narrative is told by an outsider who tells of what *he* or *she* did.

Napoleonic Wars The series of wars fought between France under Napoleon Bonaparte, and England, Prussia, Russia and Austria, between 1799 and 1815.

Paradoxical Combining apparently contradictory elements. In *Wuthering Heights*, paradox is used to suggest the coming together of opposites such as pleasure and pain, life and death.

Prodigy A child of unusual talents, beyond its years.

Romantic Part of a movement in European art, music and literature in the late eighteenth and early nineteenth centuries, showing an emphasis on feeling and content rather than order and form. Romantic writers such as Wordsworth, Coleridge, Byron, Shelley, Keats and Blake concentrated on the divine, the supernatural and the exotic, and advocated free expression of the passions and of individuality.

Saga A long, complex story, weaving together many characters and events.

Three volume novel The usual format for a published novel until the end of the nineteenth century. *Jane Eyre* appeared in three volumes. *Wuthering Heights* (two) and *Agnes Grey* (one) made up a three volume set.

List of dates

1777	Patrick Brontë born in County Down, Ireland.
1783	Maria Branwell born in Cornwall.
1802–06	Patrick studies at St. John's College, Cambridge.
1806	Ordained in London.
1806–15	Curate in Essex, Shropshire and Yorkshire.
1811	Published *Cottage Poems*.
1811–15	Curate at Hartshead, Yorkshire.
1812	Marries Maria Branwell at Guiseley, near Leeds.
1814	Maria born.
1815	Elizabeth born. Family move to Thornton, near Bradford.
1816	April 21: Charlotte born.
1817	June 26: Patrick Branwell born.
1818	July 30: Emily Jane born.
1820	January 17: Anne born.
	Patrick appointed Perpetual Curate at Haworth.
	April: family moves to the Parsonage, Haworth.
1821	September: Maria, the children's mother, dies. Elizabeth Branwell (aunt) moves to Haworth.
1825	Tabitha Aykroyd (Tabby) employed as servant. The four girls attend Cowan Bridge School.
1825	Deaths of Maria and Elizabeth.
1826	Branwell receives the toy soldiers that start the children's "scribblemania."
1827–31	The *Glasstown Saga* begins. Miniature magazines produced.
1831	Charlotte goes to school at Roe Head.
1833–35	Charlotte and Branwell begin the *Angrian Saga*. Emily and Anne work on *Gondal Saga*.
1834	Branwell's portrait of his sisters.
1835	Charlotte, as teacher, and Emily go to Roe Head.
1836	Emily's first recorded poem.
1836–37	Branwell writes to Wordsworth, and Charlotte to Robert Southey.

1838	Charlotte leaves Roe Head. Emily goes to Law Hill School to teach.
1839	Anne and Charlotte work as governesses.
1840	Branwell works as a railroad clerk. Anne goes to Thorp Green as a governess.
1841	Sisters plan to open a school.
1842	Charlotte and Emily go the Heger School in Brussels. Branwell dismissed from railroad. Death of Aunt Branwell.
1843	Charlotte's lonely year in Brussels.
1844	Writes love letters to M. Heger.
1845	Charlotte finds Emily's poems: plan for joint publication.
1846	*Poems* by Currer, Ellis and Acton Bell. All three sisters prepare novels. Charlotte begins *Jane Eyre*.
1847	October: *Jane Eyre* published. December: *Wuthering Heights* and *Agnes Grey* published.
1848	June: *The Tenant of Wildfell Hall* published. September 24: Death of Branwell. December 19: Death of Emily.
1849	May 28: Death of Anne. October: *Shirley* published.
1850	Charlotte meets Elizabeth Gaskell.
1853	January: *Villette* published.
1854	Marriage of Charlotte to Arthur Bell Nicholls.
1855	March 31: Death of Charlotte.
1857	Elizabeth Gaskell's *Life of Charlotte Brontë* published. *The Professor* published.
1860	*Emma* (novel fragment) published.
1861	June 7: Death of Patrick Brontë.

Further Reading

The works
The important novels, as well as several collections of poems and early writings, are published in hardcover and paperback in various American editions.

The lives
GASKELL, E. *The Life of Charlotte Brontë* (1857, Penguin 1975)

GERIN, W. *Charlotte Brontë: The Evolution of Genius* (Oxford, 1987)

LANE, M. *The Brontë Story* (Fontana, 1969)

POLLARD, A. *The Landscape of the Brontës* (Michael Joseph, 1988)

SPARK, M. (ed) *The Brontë Letters* (Macmillan, 1966)

WILKS, B. *The Brontës* (Peter Bedrick, 1986)

Background and criticism
ALEXANDER, C. *The Early Writings of Charlotte Brontë* (Blackwell, 1983)

ALLOTT, M. (ed) *Emily Brontë* and *Charlotte Brontë* in Casebook series (Macmillan, 1986)

EVANS, B. and G. *The Scribner Companion to the Brontës* (Scribner, 1982)

EWBANK, I. S. *Their Proper Sphere – A Study of the Brontë Sisters as Early Victorian Female Novelists* (Arnold, 1966)

MARTIN, R. B. *The Accents of Persuasion – Charlotte Brontë's Novels* (Faber & Faber, 1966)

NESTOR, P. *Female Friendship and Communities: Charlotte Brontë, George Eliot, Elizabeth Gaskell* (Oxford, 1986)

PINION, F. B. *A Brontë Companion* (Macmillan, 1975)

RATCHFORD, F. *The Brontës Web of Childhood* (Columbia University Press, 1949)

Further Information

The Brontë Parsonage Museum, Haworth, Keighley, West Yorkshire BD22 8DR, England. (The family house, now the center for Brontë studies.)
The Brontë Society, founded in 1893, runs the Museum and produces many guidebooks and postcards.

Index

111

Picture acknowledgments

The author and publishers would like to thank the following for allowing their illustrations to be reproduced in this book: Bridgeman Art Library 77; By permission of the British Library 26, 48, 59; Brontë Parsonage Museum 6, 9, 10, 12, 13, 15, 16, 18, 19, 20, 21, 23, 24, 28, 29, 30, 33, 34, 35, 37, 39, 43, 45, 46, 47, 50, 51, 52, 58, 61, 62, 64, 68, 70, 79, 80–1, 83, 85, 86, 88, 89, 94, 95, 97, 98, 99, 100, 101, 102; Fritz Eichenburg 65, 67; Mary Evans Picture Libary 11, 17, 36, 40, 41, 42, 54, 57, 87, 91, 93; National Film Archive 71, 72, 75, 76; National Portrait Gallery 31, 56.